AF334949

LITTLE-DOG-OF-IRON
by
Philip St. Clair

Ahsahta Press

Boise State University
Boise, Idaho

Some of these poems first appeared in **Ariel**, **Green's Magazine**, **Naked Man**, **New Kent Quarterly**, **Permafrost**, **Poetry Northwest**, **Prairie Fire**, **Pudding**, **Taproot**, **Término**, **Texas Review**, and **Word Loom**.

Editor for Ahsahta Press: Tom Trusky

ISBN 0-916272-29-X

Library of Congress Catalog Card Number:
85-72152

For Harv

Contents

Introduction

When wandering *homo sapiens* crossed the Bering land bridge five hundred centuries ago, doubtless one of the first creatures to note this new presence in the hemisphere was *Canis latrans,* Old Man Coyote. Coyote no doubt found the sight of these featherless bipeds highly amusing. Consider: a creature so slow it cannot run down a rabbit, but must throw stones and sticks; a creature with no proper pelt of its own, but must wrap its ungainly self in skins it has stolen from other animals; a creature whose pups take years to wean; a creature with small teeth and no claws; a creature lacking even the simple dignity of a tail. Coyote is still laughing.

I was born and raised in West Texas, and the first wild creature I ever knew, aside from birds, was Coyote through his nightly singing. Long before I saw deer or antelope or the Old Man himself, I knew the song—wild, familiar, and comforting. In those years I did not think much on Coyote's life; he was out there in the desert, within calling range of town. I didn't know he was a shape-shifter and linguist who frequented The Alcazar in Ciudad Juarez to play with the *porron* bottle, who knew all the strippers at the *Guadalajara de la Noche,* and who, I believe now, was the skinny kid with hairy wrists who sat next to me in Haldeen Braddy's History of the Language course. There was a lot I didn't know in those days.

Back in the twisted sixties, Coyote founded his own ***Journal***, which not long ago started up from its coffin and celebrated life in death once more. Poets have enjoyed his company and made up lies and truths about him ever since he first talked them into chewing a little datura to brighten their lives. It is not that Coyote became a famous personage because of the poets; did Napoleon need poets or the hundred fifty-four biographers? No, Coyote, like Hamlet, *became* the poets. Or at least he became one poet, Philip St. Clair.

Little-Dog-Of-Iron might be sub-titled The True History of Coyote In Our Times, for St. Clair reveals Coyote in his historically American manifestations, from folk hero-demon to law student, from relisher of field-mice canapes to lecher-philosopher. From hunter to hunted, in a fundamentally slapstick universe. For however plaintive Old Man Coyote's cry sounds in the desert night, there is laughter and foolishness coiled in it like snakes wintering in a ball, but laughter and tears are brothers, and Coyote was at Wounded Knee and watched with sadness as Wovoka's dream mutated and betrayed the dreamers. The ghosts dance in Coyote's memory, and we share for the moment the melancholy of immortality. The poems in ***Little-Dog-Of-Iron*** reflect the dazzling patchwork of experience that is Coyote's life and observations. Philip St. Clair presents the reader with a

collection of richly worked poems utilizing Coyote as vehicle in which the
tenor is as age-old as the animal spirit which burns in the human heart and
mind. Coyote has never sung better.

Howard McCord
Bowling Green, Ohio
August, 1985

Coyote Paranoia

The first time I came east
I was wonderfully afraid. All those trees
Made me that way. They fed at the place
Where earth and sky meet. Their seeds
Clotted wind. They tore clouds.
They fought the sun each day he rose.

Squirrels bit up my heart:
Yellow teeth the ribs of dead Brothers.
Sleek tails the thighs of young girls.
Birds flicked their heads at me and spat.
Their wings were the color of rot.
They swooped close. They pecked my lips.

I almost starved there.
Deer were silver laughing women: they all knew
I hunted alone. Rabbits changed to toads
Between my jaws. Eyes of mice
Gleamed through poison thorns. Only the snakes
Offered themselves to me.

Right on the edge
I found a white house. It was guarded
By a magic square of lawn. Seven trees
Dozed in the yard: their feet were chained
By small white stones. They didn't cry out
As I ran in the carport.

I ate the garbage. I ate the cats.
I saved the head of the friendliest cat
And laid it on the hood of a Buick
Where my delivering spirits would see it.
Then I sat down. I took my ease.
I threw out a loud prayer of thanksgiving.

I ran back in the forest as white men
Shot up my howls. All the wicked trees
Scraped my fine coat. Drab knifebirds
Plucked my lush tail. By the time
I made it to the plains of Ioway
I had no hair. I had no hair at all.

Coyote Cantina

In the long shadows of morning
The spry white man with thick glass eyes
Jogs two miles to the general store.
He shouts his list to girls with ratted hair
And they shout back. He is deaf.
There is nothing he wishes to hear.

In the quiet of early evening
He looks outside. He comes outside.
He opens a faucet by his cellar door.
He runs fresh water in a dented pan.
We hear that sound in the wind at night.
We taste that wind, and we grow restless.

We move like heat as we come down.
One by one our thirsty muzzles go
Deep in the gift—his house
Is still and dark, and the moon
Shines in his heavy eyes as he watches,
Holding his breath as he watches.

He tells loud stories about us
To the girls with ratted hair:
Soon they will part curtains
In their snug houses, their rouge
Will flavor air, and they will watch us—
Thirsty, restless, waiting a turn to drink.

Virtual Coyote

This winter there were mice
Waiting to happen. When they did
That sound was gray bone cracking,
And I smelled hot flint.
I heard many tiny claws
Where no grass grows, in the open place
In front of my den. First I thought
Spirit tossed them there for me.

These mice were not ghost-mice: I saw
No thing through them. They ran
Crooked and quick. Their eyes
Were dancing buckshot. Snowflakes
Nested in their whiskers and their tails
Struck sparks on rock. When I caught them
I threw them to the air in joy—
I tasted gall and musty fur.
I tasted warm red salt.

I know there are coyotes
Waiting to happen. God will clap hands
And they will come. They will show up
In mid-lope—many young white sheep
Will hide in fat clouds and tremble.
I wait for my virtual Brothers—their coats
Are iron and brass, and pale blue fire
Glints under their paws, and their daughters
All will want to mate with me.

Coyote Automobiles

The first car to buy me was a three-twenty-seven:
Best Chevy engine ever made. Lights,
Cops boiled in confusion and rage: I left them
Panting, I left them standing still;
There was much good mirth in the deep chuckle
Billowed from the manifold's throat
Down out the muffler. I had my name painted
On the sleek yellow door—little dashes
Around it, front and back. Like in the books.

Then there was the four-oh-nine. Songs from radios
Gave it power as it rode in sevens and tens
Out of Detroit. The first time I opened it
Was at a slow light; eyeless cops faced me
And were beside me. I romped it three times hard
And a quarter-mile down all valves
Blew off. They wrote me up; they were grinning;
Slim blue ballpoints whirred and rustled
As a towtruck gouged my chrome.

The four-eleven scared me. It was green
With gold metalflecks and looked like a box
Made of snakes. I never floored it.
When I got in and turned the silver key
Death ground his teeth in my ear.
My life belonged to many insurance devils.
Then one night some punk hot-wired it
To die in flames. And God spoke, saying,
"By the hand of the thief art thou delivered."

Coyote Divination

Once a woman came to me, saying,
Brother, listen: troubled my mind is;
My spirit is as charred, broken wood
Beneath a cold kettle. My husband's eye
Dances no more as I braid my hair—
His gaze is distant as I part my thighs
Beneath the blanket.

Continue to listen!
Tell me if my husband is unfaithful.
Tell me if I should cast him
Away from the warmth of my breasts.
Tell me if he waits by the river
For other women. Tell me if
He trades for beads and silver cones
To give other women.

Then I rose, and took down my bundle,
And unwrapped the prairie-dog skins,
And spread the set of cards inside,
Singing all the while in the high voice:

Look there! This card
Is your card—the Mourning Woman,
Weeping in her hands. Here the Man-Who-Grins,
Whose arms are full of trophies, whose heart
Is cruel and small. And here the Moon,
Where you and I cry out to the stars,
Kept apart by a trail of yellow light
Running from the heavens to the sea.
Here the Emperor of Brass, whose feet
Are rifle-barrels, whose power is as the ram
That ruts on barren crags. And here
The Generous Warrior, who fills the bowl
Of the widow and old one. And here
The False Lover, whose cedarwood flute
Charms many young virgins.

Then

(For the sun was down) I closed my tent
And made a small fire. I gave her
Corn and beans and coffee—
I touched her face. She took me in her arms,
And after we had spent and rested,
We walked together in the cool night air,
And when I lay with her again
By the long gray road of iron,
I heard a whistle walk up blue mountains.

Coyote Repose

Fat wool blankets in my winter den
Mate as I sleep. They twist in thick ropes,
Then doze at my side. I think they are snakes:
The male is red and gold and blue;
The female gray.

My jaws hurt when I wake. My last wife said
I ground my teeth. She said it was
The torture of rock. She said it was
The flint beak of a great quartz owl
Chewing weasels and ice.

She also said I thrashed and snored.
She said I lay on my side, working my legs
Like a whining, twitching rubber dog.
She said I choked on night, that my throat
Was a rattle of spit.

Now I sleep alone. Sometimes I dream
Of a blonde woman, dressed in blue fire.
She has deep breasts, firm eyes, wide hands.
She brings me a box of cheesecake
And many cigarettes.

Then my jaws and my paws are still.
Then I do not snore. And when I wake
The air is hazy-blue and sweet crumbs
Fill my whiskers and my blankets
Lie on my chest like lawn.

Coyote Fatalism

Until that day,
I keep both hill and low place
Mine: no creature usurps me
From my den by the river.
I toss plump mice
To the air; my sport is great
And my woman sleek; my pups
Honor my name to the Grandfathers.

> For no hunter may kill me:
> Their bullets fall short; their traps
> Shatter about my ankles; their poison
> Gives me laughter and dancing;
> They name me Little-Dog-Of-Iron.

On that day
Death will take me by the leg
And stop my heart. My wife
Will keen and rock; my pups
Will gash their arms with knives;
The Grandfathers will gallop
Toward me on clouds
And wash my spirit with singing.

> Then all hunters will see
> My body turn to water:
> I will eddy under the heels
> Of their black boots, and they will
> Name me Earth-Has-Drunk-Him-Up.

Coyote and the Shadow-People

from a story told by Wayilatpu of the Nez Percé

Not yesterday, not yesterday,
But a long time ago, my wife and I ran happy
Over rolling green hills, and we grew sleek
From much good game, and we longed for clumsy pups
To run with us and chew upon our ears.

But soon her yellow eyes went dim:
She lay on her side, unable to rise,
Unable to eat. When her dry tongue
Lolled in the dust, I lay down beside her—
Then she breathed no more.

I threw out a cry to the lap of the moon:
Tears caked my fur with salt;
My chest ached from sorrow. For three days
I sat and wept and howled, and on the morning
Of the fourth I heard a voice, saying,

Little Brother! Do you pine for your wife?
Yes, friend, I said, although I could not see him.
Listen, he said. I am the Spirit of Death—
I will take you to the place where she has gone.
Walk with me and I will take you there.

Continue to listen! If you walk with me,
You must do exactly as I say.
Do not be foolish! Do not be reckless!
You must promise this before we leave.
Yes, friend, I answered, What else can I do?

As the sun throbbed in the belly of the sky
We began to cross a plain. I looked to my left
And saw him as shadow, floating over the ground,
Floating by my side. Little Brother, he said,
See all the fine horses, kicking up dust

By the low hills! There must be a big roundup.
There must be many people, herding many fine horses!
Yes, friend, I said, although I could see nothing,
The horses are very fine. There are many horses,
Making much dust by the small hills.

As the sun began to ripen for night,
Spirit said, Little Brother, we are almost there.
I looked to my left, and saw his shadow
Deepen: his eyes, his long white teeth
Burned in his face. He said, Look, Little Brother,

See all the serviceberries! Let us stop and pick.
Reach up as I reach; pull down branches; eat.
This I did, although I could see nothing,
And I lifted empty paws and chewed the air.
I ran my tongue across my lips and grinned.

Spirit said, What good berries! How sweet they are!
Now my thirst is gone—what good berries they are!
Although I'd eaten nothing, I said, yes, friend,
They have quenched our strong thirst—
How good it is that we have found them!

Soon we arrived at the middle of the plain.
Spirit said, Now we have come to the long lodge
Of the dead. Your wife is here somewhere—wait,
And I will ask someone. And then I sat and waited
Under the boiling sun—for what else could I do?

In a little while Spirit returned, saying, Little Brother,
They have told me where your wife is. This is the door
Through which we will enter, and your wife is by it,
Waiting. Now do everything you see me do.
Now raise the doorflap; bend down low; enter.

This I did: although I could see nothing,
Ten paces I took, and Spirit said, Behold your wife!
How glad she is to see you! And I looked all about,
And I saw the moon, and I saw black mountains
In the west, but I did not see my wife.

Then Spirit said, Look, Little Brother,
See all the food she has set before us!
Are you not hungry? Come, Little Brother,
Let us sit by her fire and eat.
And so I did—for what else could I do?

Then Spirit sat down, and began to eat—
I did the same, although I could see nothing.
And Spirit finished, saying, What good food!
And I answered, saying, Yes, friend,
It is good that we have eaten!

Then I heard many whispers, many low voices.
Many fires blossomed before my eyes.
Many people were sitting beside them.
I saw all my friends who had gone. I saw the lodge
Reach past my sight to the mountains in the west.

Then I looked round again, and I saw my wife,
And my heart grew healthy and red,
And a great brave joy reeled my brain:
I took her close to me. I wept. I laughed.
I looked into her face a long long time.

Soon we rose from the fire to stretch,
And we walked up and down the great lodge,
Talking to all the friends who had gone.
Oh, how we feasted from the bowls of loved ones!
Oh, how we sang and danced!

Then Spirit came back to us, saying,
Little Brother, our night is coming soon.
Then you will not see us at all.
But do not leave us. You must stay right here,
And in the evening you will see our lodge again.

Then the sun rose, and my wife and friends
Faded away before my eyes. Then the heat came:
My throat was cracked from thirst; blue fire
Danced before my eyes. But I stayed there, waiting:
For what else could I do?

All through the burning day I suffered: then,
As night ran toward me from the east,
The lodge took shape. My wife
And all my friends were there just as before,
And I threw out loud cries of happiness.

Three days and nights I dwelled there on the plain:
By day, the sun threw fire at me; by night
I took my ease in the place of the dead.
But then, on the fourth day, when the lodge rose up,
Spirit came to me, saying,

Little Brother, it is time for you to leave.
It is time for you to leave with your wife
And go back to the land of the living.
Spirit, Spirit, I cried, my heart is full here—
I wish to stay here with my wife and my friends.

But Spirit said, Little Brother, that cannot be.
You must leave tomorrow. You must start your journey
Tomorrow. You must travel five days.
You must cross five mountains. Listen well—
Now I advise you on what you are to do.

Tomorrow at sunrise your wife walks with you,
But you must never, ever touch her.
You may look at her, you may speak with her,
But you must never, ever touch her.
Do not be reckless! Continue to listen!

When you cross the fifth mountain,
And descend from its crags to the plains beneath,
Only then may you do whatever you please.
Yes, friend, I answered, but my heart was dark—
How else could I feel?

When dawn came, we began to walk.
Although I could not see her, I felt her presence
As she walked behind me. Each long day
We crossed a great mountain; each cold night
We camped at the foot of its far slope.

Each night we camped, my wife was less a ghost—
Darkness faded in her pretty eyes.
The fur on her flanks grew glossy and soft.
Her breath stroked me as she ate by the fire.
Her sighs thrilled me as she drifted into sleep.

And on the fourth night, as we camped by the fire,
A passion struck me through the loins—I rose
And reached for her. What else could I do?
She cried out in a loud voice, Stop, husband, stop!
Do not touch me!

And when I took her close
She vanished, flying far away across the mountains,
Back to the land of the Shadow-People.
And the Spirit of Death flew into my tent,
And he was angry and full of rage, and he cried out

Foolish Coyote! Reckless Coyote!
See what you have done! You did not remember!
You did not obey me! See what you have done!
You, Coyote, were the first one back from death.
You, Coyote, were to make a trail from death.

See what you have done!
Soon, very soon the Human Beings will come:
Now there can be no way back for them.
Now death must be this way forever—
No way back from the long lodge of shadows!

Then I fell to the ground, and I moaned
And howled, and my tears turned the dust to mud
Beneath my face. All night long I lay there,
Weeping, begging the Spirit of Death
To lead me back to the long lodge of shadows.

When the sun came back, I began to walk.
Soon I came to the place of the horses,
And (although I could see nothing) I cried out,
Such a great roundup by the low hills!
So many people! So many horses!

Then I came to the place of the berries,
And (although I could see nothing) I reached
To pull down branches, and I cried out,
So many sweet, ripe berries! How good it is
That I have found them here!

Then I came to the place of the long lodge,
And (although I could see nothing) I raised the flap,
And bent low, and stepped in, and sat down.
I cried out, So much good food my wife has made!
How happy I am to be here, eating!

And then the sun went down, and I looked all about:
No lodgepoles reached to the mountains. No fires
Flared up in the night. So I stayed there and wept—
What else could I do? And the Spirit of Death
Never came back, and I never saw my wife again.

—*Based on a story collected by Archie Phinney in 1929.*

Coyote on Retreat

I have been with a woman for two days
And I have not eaten. I live on her juices
And the television. I place a red sign
On the door of my room: no one will enter
Unless bearing pizza.

          I say this is fasting
Done down grand style. If this were
The way of old ones all young men
Would revel in vision and long dusty hair.

After a session she lies on me
And sometimes I am in her halfway. I watch
Money shows and old movies and they are beginning
To shine from the floor. My last meal
Was beans and pills.

          My money comes
On heavy paper I am not permitted
To fold. The holes in it are square, sacred:
This is the way of the state of South Dakota.

I am not yet ready to eat. I wait to see
I Love Lucy who loves no one. Her lust
For gray fur is writ on a gray heart.
Her low shoe is quick. Her mouth lacks dignity.

Whatever I'm doing is half done. Soon
My voice will be light—I'll call up
Red medicine wheels: 'shrooms, sausage,
Olives, green peppers, and two kinds cheese.

Coyote at Second and Thirteenth

On August nights the great Tooth-Mask-House
Is lit up for Spirit: this is a good time for me,
And my friends at the Aguilar Grocería
Lounge outside playing dominoes, singing

> *Con los ojos de la plata*
> *Y dientes de la lun',*
> *Todas chiquitinas aman*
> *El Coyote-Tiburón.*

Sometimes they give me a copper token
And I ride under the ground, where a long peace belt
Links the Island in friendship. There young girls
In short print dresses admire me, singing

> *Cuando curas jueguen naipes*
> *Y dueñas beben ron,*
> *Escribimos cartas dulces*
> *Al Coyote-Tiburón.*

I walk right up to the Tooth-Mask-House
And raise my head. My throat is straight.
I get dizzy from all the power there!
I hear the men who talk to themselves singing

> *Se dice que es gran tonto*
> *Y tambien un gran ladrón,*
> *Pero esperamos siempre*
> *Por Coyote-Tiburón.*

The great shining Mask is upside down:
This is so Spirit may better see it.
Sometimes the many rows of bright teeth
Frighten me, but I sing out in a loud voice:

> *Con los ojos de la plata*
> *Y dientes de la lun',*
> *Todas chiquitinas aman*
> *El Coyote-Tiburón.*

Coyote Hitchhikes the Suburbs

This is what comes from avoiding women
With loud children—a night ride
In a pious stranger's truck. In his cab
There is no small talk. The only light
Is on his cigarette.

He knows about Jesus,
Who will lever him out of his Dodge
Come rapture-day. All his neighbors,
The jealous sinners, will gape and whine
As he soars home.

I watch my head
Glide over fine houses. I see many cats.
They are oily, indolent, secure. They nest
By tinted windows. They stare at traffic.
They brood and grin.

All televisions are on.
I think they keep the ghosts of cats,
Hardhead cats who dove through picture tubes
After the light. Now they cry to women
Who cannot hear them.

Grandfathers!
Keep me far from all light-eaters,
The ones who seek yet do not embrace,
The ones who live in cold, clear fire
And move alone.

Elegy for Kelly Keen

slain by my Brothers the Coyotes
in her third year

Upwardly mobile, your mother and father
Took over a house and a concrete slab
On the well-mowed edge of Glendale.

My Brothers watched fat moving vans
Loom in and out of your driveway
Like buffalo. They saw the chain

Around your garbage can. Your cat
And the pudgy little sausage-dog
Never came outside. But you,

Brave, naive, bright with human eyes
That stare down all creation,
Toddled under the August sun

While Brothers drifted back and forth
Among the low suburban hills—
Hungry, crooning gently, watching.

And when they danced into your yard
Singing, making the wary circle,
You must have laughed and reached to pet:

A blood remembrance of that ancient bond
Between your kin and mine. "Pretty!"
They said, and then they took you down.

Coyote in Law School

When I was in law school I had hair.
I had a lot of hair. I smoked good weed
And I drank white wine. All my dorm friends
Were very careful cynics—their parents
Lived on other planets. All my dorm friends
Tacked photos at the edges of their mirrors:
On the left side was the car.
On the right side was the girl.

Lyndon Baines Johnson gave me a grant.
When I read his letter, I grabbed my Astros hat
And hitchhiked for three days—total joy!
I sang a Lyndon Baines Johnson song
Eight hundred times—eyes of truckers sparkled
As I sang it. Bright motes of dust made diners
Holy places: young waitresses smiled at me
And waved their long red fingernails at me.

Crastino et de caetero, I did it to my head—
I found all law is owning all the land.
I learned to draw a magic square with chalk
And how to step inside. "Droit-droit!" I shouted
When termors, purlieus, warnoths menaced me.
Grandfather spat whenever I came home. Grandmother
Wept and rocked, crying, "Little owl, little owl,
Your tongue brings the whirlwind, little owl!"

Coyote Addresses His Brothers the Wolves and the Foxes

on the Banks of the Cuyahoga below
Council Rock: August 1780

In spring, when the world opened
Like a shy, pretty bride in a good blanket,
The Shawnee and Wyandot sought out a White:
A killer of children. A killer of women.
His name was Samuel Brady.

Brady laughed at them; he was a mocker;
Many young men bit into their hearts;
Their brows were coals of anger;
All of them were sullen, narroweyed;
They walked at night when no moon was.

Then twelve of that black-painted number
Found Brady and five others
Camped by a morning fire, eating, heavy
With bearmeat and bread and rum.
Quickly there was fighting: the Whites,

Dazed, bloody, ran away. But Brady
Taken was, and the chests of the young men rose:
They found ease. They took good trophies:
They took his rifle of the many brass fittings.
They took his knife of the coffin-handle.

They spared him for a long torture.
They bound him upright in their camp,
Saying, Brother, now we go for venison,
For the meat of great rejoicing,
For the feast to honor your pain.

Brother, prepare your journey westward.
There the sun sets, and there spirits go
When they rise up from the body. Then Brady wept,
Streaking his face. Then Brady fouled
His lower garment and was dishonored.

The young men left to hunt, and Brady wailed
To his Jesus, saying, Jesus, O deliver me
From my captors who will kill me slowly.
Deliver me, and I will be a better one:
My voice will always be a hawk to heaven.

Then a young girl, who was simple,
Ran to the Brady with a knife, saying,
I shall cut thongs; I shall cut ropes;
I shall give you to your legs and feet—
Away you may run to your Nation.

Then Brady stood free at the stake,
And Evil One's voice nested in his ears,
And all the good talk at the White Jesus
Fell to the ground as the tight-hulled chestnut
That will not sprout.

Then Brady seized a large rock,
And brought it down on the girl's neck,
And she fell to the ground, and blood
Came out her mouth, and her spirit flew
Away from the top of her head, and Brady ran.

When the young men returned, rage
Drove their eyes to the socket's rim:
They ran the prints of Brady's feet;
They spoke not to the other; their tongues
Were stiff with hatred.

Soon Brady heard them running, for he
Was slow in his boots, and rum-drinking
Had wasted his heart and his lungs.
Then the Nation of Rabbits, the swift ones,
The small tricksters, the good jokers,

Cried out to him, saying, Brady Brady Brady,
Run to the river where the rocks
Form ledges, where hemlocks join over water:
There the river narrows; there you may leap it;
There the way is to your safety.

Then many Rabbits ran past him
To litter the ground with droppings.
Brady slipped many times; Brady fell many times;
His face and elbows were bruised; his mouth
Brimmed with curses and wickednesses.

The Rabbits laughed, and covered that laughter
With front paws. Brady Brady Brady, they cried,
Run faster, lest your enemies capture you;
Lest your enemies torture you; lest your enemies
Give your manhood to the knives of women.

The Rabbits cried, Between two great hemlocks
The river narrow is: jump to the far side.
Then Brady stopped for breath, and saw
The distance over that swift river
As the length of four men.

Then Brady turned, and ran the other way,
And saw the young men coming. Then Brady turned
And ran the other way, and reached the place
Of the hemlocks, and threw his body
Over the river.

Now the Nation of Rabbits had covered the far side
With droppings: when Brady fell there
His hands knew no purchase; he struggled
On the face of dark rock. One young man said,
White men mate with stone and mosses.

One young man shot three bolts
Running-heart quick:
A shaft cut Brady's hand. A shaft
Grazed Brady's coat. A shaft
Lodged deep in the cheek of Brady's rump.

Brothers! You have seen the wounded catamount
Snarl and twist and knot about the spear
That pins him; I say the Brady
So wept and swore and groveled on that rock
Those young men laughed.

Then Brady limped to Deep Lake, not far
From the river. His blood made good tracking,
So the young men took their time. They laughed
And walked proudly, for the setting sun
Was a mirror of bronze on their adornments.

When they reached the edge of the lake,
The lake where ancient fish lie very still,
The lake of secrets, the lake of no bottom,
They saw nothing but reeds. One said,
In the water he hides; let us watch for him

As Heron waits for Frog. They sat down.
They took ease. Night came, and some said,
Brady is dead in that water; we shall go back.
Some said, Brady yet lives; he breathes in water;
A sly one he is; we shall wait him through.

When morning came, all the young men
Talked with each other, saying, Brady is dead:
Now fishes will eat his fat tongue;
Now muskrats will use his fingerbones
For trinkets and for gaming-pieces.

Brothers, hear me—Brady escaped.
Whites say he hid beneath a log, drawing in air
By the feet of young men. This may be.
But I think Evil One, who revels in bad thought,
Heard Brady as he made his mouth for death.

I think Brady was snatched by Evil One
And taken far down in the ground.
I think they addressed each other
In the high voice. I think they embraced
And shared food. I think they are Brothers.

Now White men give Brady great honor.
Now he is called Captain-Over-The-Others.
At the tavern and church is he praised
By all the White men—all the White women
Fashion garments for his person.

Their children have a game: they leap small brooks
As others chase them. They fire muskets of wood.
They crouch in tall grass and breathe through
Hollow rushes. They shriek, and they play at war,
And no Red child may run with them.

Coyote Horny

New in town and cravin' a little strange,
I went to the Holiday Inn: the lounge
Was almost empty but for one brunette,
Kinda stringy in the throat, all alone
At the end of the bar. She had
Fine legs and big tits. She said
She used to be a stewardess but her ear
Kept on gettin' popped over La Guardia
So she had to let that go. After that
She was a cocktail waitress but got herself
In dutch with a touchie-feelie boss
So she had to let that go too. I said
I used to do a lot of stunts in Hollywood.
I said Did you see the picture
Where Tab Hunter saves Jayne Mansfield
From certain death at the hands of wild coyotes?
Well, one of them was me, I said. Then
She got kinda distant so I asked her if she'd
Like to come to my motel and trade sucks
On a quart bottle of Rebel Yell. She said
I don't fuck fur—I wear it. Then she left
And stuck me with her tab.

                              I drove downtown,
Went in a college bar. There was a band
So I had no trouble gettin' girls
To dance with me. One of them had
Fine legs and big tits. I bought her a brew
And asked What's your sign and she said
Scorpio with the moon fifteen degrees Leo
And Gemini risin'. And then I said
I was born under Peyote
When the moon was large and low
And I'm the slickest, wisest dude
That you will ever know, I said.
She said Are you holding and I said Yes.
So I sprung for another cool one and asked
What's your major and she put her hand
On my thigh and said Predator Control.

I ran in the men's room and dove straight out
The window, steppin' on some guy's head
Who was in there takin' a dump.

After I picked all the glass out my face,
I tooled over to an all-night dinette
To cool out some. The place was empty
Except for the waitress, who had
Fine legs and big tits. Normally I wouldn't
Have messed with her 'cause one eye
Was kinda holdin' a conversation with the other
But it was gettin' late. So I asked her
What her name was and she said Mabel Louise.
Then I told her that my name was Mister C
And the C stands for coffee 'cause I grind so fine.
She snickered into a paper towel so I knew
I was gettin' somewhere. We talked some more
And I waited 'til she got off and then
We went out for a drive in my 'sheen
Way out in the country. Park here,
She said, and then she took her hand
And put it on my crotch. Well,
It didn't take me long to get my britches down
And get her britches down. Then she said
Uh, do you have *it* and I said Hell no
You've got *it* in your hand. Then she said
I don't mean *that*—I've got *it*
And I think you should know. Well,
At that point the ol' Bandito de Amor
Sorta went limp so I zipped myself up
And drove her home.

                    So I went back
To my room at the Bide-A-Wee Motel,
Cracked open the jug of Rebel Yell
And settled in. I picked up the phone
And talked a little trash at the operator
But she cut me off. Then I messed with the knob
On the teevee set so that all the girls
Had fine legs and big tits. Even Joan Rivers
Had fine legs and big tits. Somewhere between
The Late and the Late-Late Show
I crashed out. I dreamed that a wall-eyed waitress

In a long gray fur coat was chasin' me
With a purse full of Compound 1080. I woke up
Screamin' at four-fifteen and not a
Goddamn thing on the tube. Well,
I was too sober to sleep so I wrapped up
In a thick blanket, sat down
Right in the middle of the floor,
And waited up for Connie Chung.

Muzak Coyote

At this truckstop four young men sing
In boxes. They croon by the table
Where waitresses watch distant hawks,
Where they lounge and listen as reedy voices
Tell the pain of loving young.

Each girl's white shoe
Carves an arc in stale air. Each yellow sole
Nods and bobs in cigarette ghosts
While out the window ripe summer wheat
Dances a victory on the broken earth
Of Valentine, Nebraska.

              I think the young men
Hurt too much, for when they make
Their saddest, highest note, many crows
Burst out of the wounded field and every waitress
Stares at me as if to take my heart.

Coyote Eucharist

Three dark powerlines link the street
To Ray's Phoenix Lounge: grackles live
Where they join. Fifty feet away
A small gray coffin hums on a pole.
My fur spikes up as I trot by.
From there each cable
Curves to the loose twig-circle
Keeping their children.

                Each day I watch
The babies fatten. They begin to glow.
They leave orange trails as they reach
To be fed: naked wings and blunt quills
Crackle, arc. Their cries flake brick,
Haze paint, turn a keen bright needle
In everyone's ear. Now all easy game
Is gone.

         They are hungry
For the fire holding home. They lean
Over the nest, cutting half-moons
In tarred arteries of light,
Pecking and scratching at crystal kettles.
Crazy-brave, they stretch to lash out
At mothers with kids, at joggers,
At utility people.

        Now the street
Is barred by yellow trestles. Neighbors
Lock their pets away—the calico cat
I want for lunch is gone. A cop and shotgun
Wait under the nest: his cruiser
Pounds my face with red and white. Dazed,
Dappled, famished, I hide here and wait
For a small bite of spark.

Coyote Surprise

All at once a yellow dream
Flies overhead—its wings
Tilt and smirk. Its tail's
The lobe of a toadstool
In a dead tree's shade.

Hunters curse and grin inside.
One wears a baseball cap
With a whiskey-name in black.
The other wears a cowboy hat
Wrapped in the skin of a snake.

Rifle slugs spackle rock
Right by my paws—engines
Braid my fur with racket.
No hawk ever tore up
God's air like that.

Grandfathers! Keep away
The sudden ghost. Keep away
Spirits of the iron feather—
Evil One's wind-brothers
In visions unannounced.

Coyote Apocalypse

The Good White Man is coming. I see him
Move in the corner of my left eye.
He gestures at me, and when I turn
He is gone. All old stories say
He carries plates of stone as Moses did
But this I have not seen. He may be Death.
He may be Death's brother. I say this because
Death comes from the left to fight
With a long red hand. All my friends
Say this is so.

                    I am waiting
For the Great Cleansing. In this I am patient
As any Christian. I am waiting for Jews
To rebuild their temple so I listen
To the radio. I am waiting for White Man
To build a dwelling high in the air
So I listen to the radio. For years
Old ones waited in small, dark houses
And thought on old stories. Now they go
Outside at night. Now they look at the sky.
Red lights gleam from their radios.

When he comes to the land he will float.
Birds will fly under his feet.
When he lifts his tablets to catch the noon sun
The world will molt like an old snake.
The wicked and thoughtless will die.
Then all will be bright with flowers,
Heavy with trees. All water
Will be sweet. Bears will fatten
On salmon and fruit. Great buffalo nations
Will tremble the ground and every red radio
Will vanish in smoke.

Coyote Addresses His Brothers
The Wolves and the Foxes

on the Banks of Wounded Knee Creek:
April 1891

Brothers! When the great chief Sitting Bull
Heard of a new religion, brought down from heaven
By the Prophet Wovoka, his heart grew light:
He wished to hear more. He summoned
Kicking Bear, who had gone to find that magic,
Who had learned it from the Blue Cloud nation.

And Kicking Bear spoke to the people,
And told them of the world to come,
And reunion with their ancestors,
And the death of every white man,
And the singing and the dancing
Jesus taught him up in heaven.

And Kicking Bear walked among them
To give them the dance and the singing,
And they joined hands and made a circle,
And their steps were slow and careful,
And their dancing moved as the sun moves,
Going from the right hand to the left.

They worshipped far into the darkness:
Many fell down and had visions,
And were taken up to Wakan Tanka.
When Little Wound went up to heaven,
Jesus met him, and embraced him as Brother,
And led him to his relatives and children,
And brought him the playmates of his youth.
When Crooked Nose went up to heaven,
Jesus told him He would save all red men,
And gave him two red berries
And two black berries, fresh from the bushes
That grow near the tent of Wakan Tanka.

On the fourth day of that dancing,
McLaughlin, the white agent at Standing Rock,
Sent fourteen men to stop it. But Spirit
Clouded their minds, and sent them back:
They were as men who walk within their sleep.
But the eleven who came after
Rode horses straight into the circle—
They seized Kicking Bear and all his men
And led them off the reservation.

That night, before a new dancing,
Sitting Bull went into his cabin,
And brought out a fine long pipe,
Kept in remembrance of the day
He brought his people home
From Grandmother's Land, five winters after
The fight at the Little Big Horn.
He raised that pipe, and with his hands
He broke it in two, saying,
"For the words of the Messiah,
For the world Great Holy promised,
For the coming of our ancestors,
For the death of all the white men,
I will fight and die!"

And the new way threw down deep roots
In all the agencies, and at Pine Ridge
There was much dancing, and many red men,
Arrogant in the faith, waved bright knives
At white men, and sold what they had to buy guns,
And wore blue ghost-shirts that were proof
Against white bullets. Then the talking papers
Cried out, saying that a great battle
Was surely to come, and white men at Washington
Turned their eyes westward.

And white men at Pine Ridge made threats:
They vowed to stop the issue of beef
And the dancers grew afraid.
Then Short Bull had a vision
And addressed the faithful, saying,

"Brothers, listen! A great tree will sprout
On the banks of Pass Creek, and all believers
Will see dead kinsmen by it
Waiting for the embrace. Now you must dance
For the rest of this moon, and at its end
The earth will shake, and a great wind
Will blow down from the north,
And the tree will burst from the ground
Fully leaved, and all our dead fathers
Will circle its trunk.

"Believers! Fear for nothing!
Even the guns of the white belong
To our Father in heaven—whatever they say
Do not heed them!"

When Sitting Bull heard of that vision,
He sent a message to the agency,
Saying that he must travel to Pine Ridge
To pray and dance. Then McLaughlin
Gave the order to arrest him:
Thirty Indian Police rode into his camp
And the Army sent men to help:
One hundred soldiers kept watch a mile away,
And they had a many-barreled wagon-gun,
And they had a twice-shooting wagon-gun.

When the Indian Police rapped on his door,
Sitting Bull said, "Yes! Come in the house!"
When the Indian Police told him their mission,
Sitting Bull said, "All right!
Let me put on my clothes and go with you!"
Now the Indian Police were fearful:
They wished to leave quickly,
But Sitting Bull was slow and aged,
So they honored that great chief
By dressing him, and their hands trembled.
His youngest wife sang, "Husband!
Always you have been a brave man—
What is going to happen now?"

Soon many people at the camp
Gathered by the cabin door.

When the chief came out, two men
Held his arms; a third kept a revolver
Tight against his back. Then Crow Foot,
The son of seventeen winters, cried out:
"Father! Always you have called yourself
Great chief, but now you are being taken
By the Chests-Of-Metal!" Then Sitting Bull
Struggled with the Indian Police,
Saying in a loud voice: "All right!
I will not go another step!" Then
Knives and rifles came out of blankets
And the people fought the Indian Police,
Driving them inside the cabin.

When a runner came with news, the Army
Galloped to the camp of Sitting Bull:
A half-mile away, they saw much smoke
And fired the twice-shooting wagon-gun—
Many died and many ran away.

Then the Army came into the camp
And saw that the ground was strewn with corpses,
And saw that Sitting Bull and his son were dead.
Across the river, a warrior in a ghost-shirt
Sang as he rode through the trees: "Father!
I thought you said we were going to live!"

Then began the capture of the dancers:
Those who fled the camp of Sitting Bull
Joined Big Foot's people, who were taken by soldiers
And brought to Pine Ridge. "It is well,"
Said Big Foot, "for I was going there anyway!"

The soldier-chiefs told all their men
To take the weapons of the faithful:
Troopers began to search each lodge.
Then the people, cold and hungry,
Gathered near the tent of Big Foot,
And they joined hands and made a circle,
And they faced inward on that circle,
And their steps were slow and careful,
And their dancing moved as the sun moves,
Going from the right hand to the left.

Then Yellow Bird, the medicine-chief,
Began to pray, throwing red dust
To the winter air, crying "Brothers!
Do not be afraid! There are many soldiers
And many bullets, but the prairie is vast—
No bullet will harm you, for as you see me
Toss up dust, and as you see dust float away,
So shall the bullets of soldiers
Be taken away by the wind of Spirit!"

And Black Coyote stood up, and drew
A fine Winchester from beneath his blanket,
Shouting that he would never give it up
Unless the white man paid for it in gold.
When two white troopers seized him from behind
Black Coyote's rifle spoke—many warriors
Fired their weapons at the lines of soldiers.

Then, my Brothers, the killing began.
That noise was like the robe of Wakan Tanka
Being torn in two. That smoke was like
A great white fist, rising in anger at the sun.

Here is the count of the faithful who died:
Of the men, eighty-four.
Of the women, forty-four.
Of the children, eighteen.
Big Foot lay dead in the snow.
Yellow Bird lay dead in his tent.
Black Coyote was never seen again.

And when Wovoka, the good prophet,
The preacher of peace and friendship
Between red man and white man,
Heard of that fight, he wept,
And pulled the blanket over his head,
Crying, "My children! My children!
Now you must travel a new path,
The only way for us to walk—
The white man's road!"

Coyote Regret

A long night is coming. Soon
My people will run in the desert, each
Aiming the throat at the stars,
Calling out in the high voice
As gophers curl to sleep and dark air
Chills.

      Old and crippled,
I will not go out. My lungs
Cough up bright blood. One ear
Drones to the other through my skull.
My paws cramp and knot. My coat
Is a threadbare blanket.

        My wife and son
Watch me, waiting for me to die. Each dawn
They leave, trotting side by side,
Talking and laughing. When they come back
They carry mice between their jaws
For me. They lay them in the dirt

And say nothing. When I talk to them
They do not answer. The eyes of my son
Are cruel and wide. The heart of my wife
Has been driven away. Then I think
On all my hard words and a ghost
Walks through me.

      Now
They go outside. I hear their voices
Rise, pause, tremble, fall. They cry
At the rabbit who sits on the moon—
My son would rip it just for his pleasure
And my wife does not care.

Coyote Cryptomnesia

Alone alone this starry night
The desert is awash with wine
The scarlet trim upon her coat
The print of lace upon her hip

Goodbye goodbye in foggy streets
That filled with rain beneath the lamp
Her saffron face her hazel eye
Her purple lips her amber comb

The wind that runs across the sea
Had mixed gray leaves within her hair
My fingers reached to ease them out
My fingers trembled searching her

The buttons on her blouse were dice
Rung out upon the cobblestones
As dice the game of corsetier
I was the gentlest of men

I turned her throat up to the light
I saw a wavelet lift her pulse
Dark blood beside her golden chain
Dark blood beneath my golden ring

She said she was a languid hand
That fed and slept within the deep
She was Anemone she said
Blue-purple russet yellow green

Goodbye goodbye to wine and stars
I hope she has forgotten me
On stars and wine she would not live
If I had taken her away

Coyote Insomnia

In this old house, sleep feints at me.
All rooms are empty save the one
I yawn in. Movie magazines
Keep my coat from the floor.
I have to sit on Norma Desmond's face.

My neck-hackles will not lie down.
My legs cramp. My dull teeth
Need good meat. My tail
Is a wounded snake in the dust.
My ears ring with many dead tongues.

Many dead hands clutch my throat.
My worst wife glares at me
To make me wince. My children
Twitch their mouths at me.
They cry, Betrayer! Betrayer!

I hear spirits rattle warped doors.
They pace between chair-shadows.
They drop coins and short pencils.
They cough into fists. They bump.
They pull down blinds at sunrise.

I shout at them down gutted halls.
I say, Spirits, spirits,
Death whips you. Death mocks you.
Death keeps you in this house
By the ghost of your purse.

I will make dancing when dawn comes.
I will circle Death and I will spit.
I will tell these spirits who they are.
Then the sun will bring us home—
Grandfathers! Spread wide the blanket!

Coyote Villanelle

Upon this ground I want to leave our mark.
A seashell lives forever, pressed in clay—
I want our tracks to touch Grandmother's heart.

God's eye is wide. He sees that light and dark
Are swifts that dive and circle after prey:
Upon this ground I want to leave our mark.

Look at this tree! Its mottled, weary bark
Is ruffled by the wind and blown away.
I want our tracks to touch Grandmother's heart.

Look at this stone! She made it when the lark
Sang over her land on the last First Day:
Upon her ground I want to leave our mark.

Soon we will die, and walk the Road of Stars—
What do we leave here if our footprints fade?
I want our tracks to touch Grandmother's heart.

Let those who come long after watch our stark
Stone testament meander in a braid—
Upon this ground I want to leave our mark.
I want our tracks to touch Grandmother's heart.

Coyote Snowbound

It is winter. The handsbreadth of fire
Warms air in the circle of skin
We have set up on the plain. Ice
Lies heavy on the flaps of our tent.

My wife sits beside me, wrapped
In her best blanket, singing a tune
She uses when her small, pretty knife
Flashes on the hide she is working.

It is strange to hear that voice
When her hands are so still, when
Her hands are hidden away,
Nested on each other like drowsy mice.

The fire rises as she stares in it.
Tonight it is her bright puppy —
Wide-eyed, eager to please, it rolls
Inside the hearth, belly up.

Her hand roams from the blanket
And lifts a thin stick. Idly,
It taps gray coals
Free of ash, baring the fire's

Red heart. The new glow
Softens her hair, and once more
She is a young girl, drawing water
With her mother and sister.

Now sleep walks toward her:
She yawns and rises. The blanket
Falls from her shoulders
And I build our fire for night.

Coyote Apophrades*

This house—built far away from town,
Abandoned when the land would give
No more. Here I hide and rest
In an empty parlor, where dead men
Will not let me sleep.

When the moon grows full I must leave:
The mirror is heavy with strangers
And the bowl by my bed tips
Out of my reach. They yank hair,
Hide food, rattle doorknobs,

Grumble in my ear. I long
For days that are gone, when spirits
Roared at me from horses of flame
And wailed through rattle and drum,
Burning away all darkness.

But tonight I'm kept awake
By anxious talk: they threaten me
With rent. They ask me
Why I've mussed a doily
On a sofa that isn't there.

The moon ripens as I lie and watch it;
The sun marches toward me
In red shoes. I wait for the good voice
At dawn. I wait for the voice to tell me
Which way to run.

*The dismal or unlucky days upon which the dead return to their former homes.

*Philip St. Clair was born in Ohio in 1944. He presently teaches at Bowling Green State University. He has written essays on frontier artist James Otto Lewis and pioneer naturalist Louis Jean Pierre Vieillot; his **Frederic Remington: The American West** was published by Bonanza Books in 1981. Collections of poetry include **In the Thirty-Nine Steps** (Shelley's, 1980) and **At the Tent of Heaven** (Ahsahta, 1984).*

Ahsahta Press

POETRY OF THE WEST

MODERN

*Norman Macleod, *Selected Poems*
 Gwendolen Haste, *Selected Poems*
*Peggy Pond Church, *New & Selected Poems*
 Haniel Long, *My Seasons*
 H. L. Davis, *Selected Poems*
*Hildegarde Flanner, *The Hearkening Eye*
 Genevieve Taggard, *To the Natural World*
 Hazel Hall, *Selected Poems*
 Women Poets of the West: An Anthology
*Thomas Hornsby Ferril, *Anvil of Roses*
*Judson Crews, *The Clock of Moss*

CONTEMPORARY

*Marnie Walsh, *A Taste of the Knife*
*Robert Krieger, *Headlands, Rising*
 Richard Blessing, *Winter Constellations*
*Carolyne Wright, *Stealing the Children*
 Charley John Greasybear, *Songs*
*Conger Beasley, Jr., *Over DeSoto's Bones*
*Susan Strayer Deal, *No Moving Parts*
*Gretel Ehrlich, *To Touch the Water*
*Leo Romero, *Agua Negra*
*David Baker, *Laws of the Land*
*Richard Speakes, *Hannah's Travel*
 Dixie Partridge, *Deer in the Haystacks*
 Philip St. Clair, *At the Tent of Heaven*
 Susan Strayer Deal, *The Dark Is a Door*
 Linda Bierds, *Flights of the Harvest-Mare*
 Philip St. Clair, *Little-Dog-Of-Iron*

*Selections from these volumes, read by their authors, are now available
 on *The Ahsahta Cassette Sampler.*